INTERROBANG

Interrobang

MARY DALTON

Signal EDITIONS

THE POETRY IMPRINT AT VÉHICULE PRESS

Published with the generous assistance of the Canada Council for the Arts and the Canada Book Fund of the Department of Canadian Heritage.

Canada Council for the Arts Conseil des arts du Canada

Canada

SIGNAL EDITIONS EDITOR: CARMINE STARNINO

Cover design by David Drummond
Photo of the author by Bojan Furst
Copyedited by Sariah Hossein
Set in Minion and Filosofia by Simon Garamond
Printed by Livres Rapido Books

Dépôt légal, Library and Archives Canada and the Bibliothèque national du Québec, third trimester 2024

Published by Véhicule Press, Montréal, Québec, Canada
www.vehiculepress.com

Distribution in Canada by LitDistCo
www.litdistco.ca

Distributed in the US by Independent Publishers Group
www.ipgbook.com

Printed in Canada on FSC certified paper.

"I" is merely one of the world's instantaneous spasms.
–Clarice Lispector, *The Passion According to G. H.*

I'm Nobody! Who are you?
Are you—Nobody—too?
Then there's a pair of us!
Don't tell! they'd advertise—you know!
–Emily Dickinson

Contents

Taking Stock

The everyday. What is most difficult to discover.
–Maurice Blanchot, "Everyday Speech"

The Shop

Again.
The lollop of the cow-bell, and
she's entering that ritual space.

Southwest corner of
a biscuit-box house:
two rooms, at once contained,
crammed and cramped, categorized—
and permeable, boundless,
reaching out, welcoming
the youngsters, the old ones,
the shambler, the steady customer,
the come-by-chance.

A node of neighbourhood.
A cornucopia, spilling over.
Old Mother Hubbard's life-saver.
An emporium of sugary bliss.

Doors open to the
clutchers of warm nickels, to
young bucks and the grizzled,
bogeyman and gargoyle,
termagant and shy ones, the
blushers and twiddlers,
the harridan, the hero, the thief.
A clearing house.

For Bay Roberts
wholesalers,

Harbour Grace,
Carbonear,
Clarke's Beach,
Spaniards Bay—
for Ackerman's and Tetford's
(*Titford's* we giggled)
a conduit of Uncle Sam's
glittering goods.

The Naming

Not *store*—that
was an outbuilding
or several,
along with stable and cellar
and brookhouse.
Not *groc and conf*—
a townie invention?

It was *the shop:*
you might be
gone up to the shop
gone out in the shop
opening the shop
tending the shop
minding the shop
closing the shop—
down on your knees
scrubbing the shop floor.

Kennedys' shop
Costigans' shop
Conrans' shop
Hawcos' shop
Walshs' shop
Terrys' shop
Daltons' shop

Like the schools,
Shamrock and St. Joseph's,
the Academy Hall,

the stables and stores,
the fishing sheds,
like a myriad modes
of coherence, communion—
all vanished.

But
you can still
mail a letter,
write a poem,
make an archive.
Get the names right.

The Shop Bell

A warm mellow tone—
lucky the cow that sported it,
ambling in meadows.

Dangling over the door,
it announces an entry,
calls her from the kitchen.

A few minutes
chewing the fat:
the weather, new baby, or
a son home from Boston.
The rhubarb just coming.

A hunk of cheddar chopped
from the block, weighed,
encased in brown paper,
white string unspooled
from its cylinder—
a twist, a flick of the wrist,
string snapped, a flourish,
hand faster than eye—
a bow—
there you go!

A customer leaving,
the bell sounds out its goodbye,
in its own way a blessing—
the transaction marked kinder

than those signalled by
church bells or school bells.

Tucked in a drawer,
the bell's flared mouth now mute—
yet it
speaks volumes, resounds.

The Money Box

Of black lacquered tin,
striped in red, gold, and silver,
it was a modest affair.

Size of a doorstopper novel,
unlocked, but lockable,
it was safe as houses.

Under the counter
it held its freight of cheques, bills,
lists of goods on tick.

It was discreet, keeping
news of unpaid bills, unkept
promises to itself.

A good steward, mum
when the folksinger fled,
trailing tunes and debt.

Open: for the priest's dues,
the car geared for a straight knee,
more stock, the doctor's fees.

Money flowed in, flowed
out; time flowed, rivered on—
water rusting the tin.

. . .

A closet, top shelf—
with scrapbooks, old quilts,
there the money box perches.

Its innards empty.

Gerald S. Doyle's Newfoundland Cod Liver Oil: The Blue Bottle

If fairies cavorted in the shop,
if the bottles and boxes
up on that tier of shelves
stirred to rampant life at night,
it would surely be the general,
stern and broad-shouldered,
flaunting his shoulder marks,
a man with a history, a mission.

Headless but haughty,
he towered over
Dr. Chase's Ointment
Bayer's Aspirin
(their modest tins)
Milk of Magnesia
Minard's Liniment
Vick's Vapour Rub
Dodds' Liver Pills.
Castor oil and olive oil,
in their see-through outfits,
were in awe of him—
he was *so pure and so strong*,
they gushed.
His blue glass gleamed.
A cold dark blue.

We dreaded him, knew
each morning, sure as

the sun rose we were in for
a spoonful of his stinking
gut-churning goodness.
Near gagging, we swallowed.

The law was the law, but
the mother showed mercy:
relief from another shop cranny.
For each: orange wedges,
juicy and ready
to cram in right after.

Capsules came later,
and still we had oranges—
though we missed the drama.

On the Bill

Then another shop
opened, just up the road;
we youngsters were all
on fire with the news.
Ice cream! He got
vats of Brookfield in stock!

So one sweltering Friday,
up I trotted—
found an excuse to leave
my mother at the counter,
list in her hand,
pencil behind her ear,
loading up cartons.

Vanilla? Strawberry?
Oh chocolate, Neapolitan!
I dithered.
Mr. Bernard was patient. At last
I settled on
a great mound of strawberry.
Thank you, I said,
as my mother had taught me,
reaching out for the cone.
A trifle grandly,
proud of my shift
from server to buyer,
I commanded,
Put that on the bill.

Of course he
gave me the cone.
And how was I to know?
That's how most folks
bought stuff in our shop.

Anti-Costco

I

SHOPPING LIST

Scrap—an envelope back—
inked in a shaky hand,
passed up over the counter
in a tiny grand-daughter's hand:

small chunk of cheese
a chicken leg
one cigarette
a piece of bologna.

What she has got
in her own cabbage garden:
carrots, lettuce, and onions,
beet for the salad.
Her grandmother's
chive patch. *Sives*,
she called them, a trace
of Channel Isles
ghosts in the name.

II

BY SIZE (RAMIFYING)

2 cents for a small apple
5 cents for a medium apple
8 cents for a very big apple

Each cosseted in its purple
crepe-paper nest, inside
its slatted pine crate—two
of which would, upended,
metamorphose into
shelves of a desk with
a plywood top varnished.

Shelves soon stocked with
Heidi
Huckleberry Finn
Little Women
Pinocchio
Robinson Crusoe
Alice in Wonderland and
Through the Looking Glass.

Fruit of the Tree
of the Knowledge
of Good and Evil.

Word had spread—
as word was wont to spread,
in that time—
sans Facebook *sans* Pinterest:
that Scotty's Chips
would ship off a book
in exchange for just fifty
potato-chip bags.

Every bow-tied black terrier
sold in that shop
found its way back
to a small reader's hands—
and the books flowed in.

All the Clubs from Holyrood to Brigus

Shadows [offer] shelter as can four walls and a roof...
–John Berger, *and our faces, my heart, brief as photos*

The Names, the Shifting

Go back far enough: *grog shop*, *shebeen*.
Then *beer parlour*, *tavern*,
followed close on by *club* and by *lounge*,
decked out in their finery.
(Not ever, ever *pub*, that townie newcomer.)

Shebeen and *still* in the days of official
constraint and thick jars of moonshine;
beer parlours when beer was all they could sell,
when the phrase reeked of scorn;
taverns also a man's domain, stinking of smoke
and loud argument, the battles of blue-collar jousters;
and in time a place for the sedate, the genteel:
Velvet Horn (Velvet Hat) with its ornate door of oak,
its couples and dress codes;
its juke-boxes and jiving; uniformed
waitresses and white napkins next door.

After a Hard Day

Oh you'll get the Miss Prisses, the ones who'll look down their noses if you drop in for a few beer. You wouldn't know but the clubs were franchises of Sodom and Gomorrah, with the Four Horsemen parked around back. I tell you, after a hard day on the construction I'm rearing to stop in here, shoot the breeze, throw a few darts. Forget the boss and the mortgage and the threat of Fort Mac. Maybe find a new woman. And my buddies'll tell you the same thing if you ask them. Cheaper than a shrink any day. And more fun, too.

Scrap of a Story

No houses there now—not for a hundred years. Hard to fathom how they could thrive down there on the Point. D'Iberville's men burnt it twice over; sheep and goats kept it close-cut. Bush and marsh and razor cliffs. And the climb to haul up the fish from the beach. Heartbreak Hill. The distances, the cracks and the crevices and the winter wind whistling through. All we've got is the scrap of a story. That night, Christmas Eve, and a blizzard. In all that weather he walked the mile up to Bid's Hill, up to Bid's shop. Was it for twine or molasses, a spin-top? Was it for grog? Did he tuck a jar under his arm? In the whirl of wind and snow he set out for the way back, but he mistook the path. Not a word was heard of him. As if he'd vanished into the funnelling storm. The wife and five youngsters waiting at home. It was the spring when they found him. A boat put out from Conception, a fellow named Trahey. He spied something dark against the melting whites of the cliff-slope. When they got to him, he was curled up like he was sleeping. His greatcoat folded under his head like a pillow.

The Honest Man

Loads more of them one time—not to mention the stills. In Holyrood alone: The Butterpot Tavern, Mother Hickey's, Mary Anne LaCour's, Davises', Fureys', Crawleys'. Not to mention the Bunker, with its secret door, its concrete walls and Sunday boozing. Some of them were oases, even if the only camels were cigarettes; a warm welcome when the world was a snarling dog at your back. Bob O'Toole's now: no fancy names—no promises and brown and dim like the rest of them—it was just Bob O'Toole's, but that's one tavern might hang out a sign, The Honest Man.

First time I went in, five or six fellows sitting around, chewing the fat, smoke thick as incense, beers on the table. No one behind the bar. I soon got the hang of it. You'd go in, saunter up to the counter, take what you wanted, keep your empties for tally. By and by Bob'd roll in—he was a bit like a ball, short and round—stroll on over, enquire in the jolliest way, "And how many beers did you have now?" He said to me once that in all the years he had the tavern he always got paid—something he couldn't brag of the groceries he sold on tick at his store over the road.

The Twillick

The Blue Moon. The Velvet Hat. The Newfoundland Lounge. They should have a bar called The Twillick. Go in there now and what you'll see is those fellows—and the women, too—home from Alberta, the SUVs and the monster trucks shining in the parking lots, and them huddled over the flash and dash, the blips and beeps of the VLTs, feeding in the dollars they left their place and young ones for, feeding in the big money they got on the planes for. The big money they sold their backs and lungs for, often as not. Or crowded round a pool-table like worshippers at one of those new-fangled centre altars, praying at the shrine of Texas Hold 'Em.

Girl at the Bar

> I spend most of my time not dying.
> That's what living is for.
> –Frederick Seidel, "Fog"

She is looking into the distance.
The light touches her forehead, her neck;
hovers about her eyes and chin,
gold strands of her hair,
gold of the beer glass.
Fiery light glances off her
hair, upswept at the back.
The busy iconography of the bar,
its framed memories and plaques,
the phone talker nearby—
against their blurry clutter
a stillness, a space at once inner
and knowing, a pool of solitude
in the whirl of the carnival.

Here, in the commotion, the crowd,
the photographer's found
a Botticelli angel,
a Vermeer beauty,
T-shirted—
yet his gaze travels further:
one senses that soon
the moment will vanish;
she will slide off the bar stool,
toss off a wisecrack,
grin at the comeback,

sashay out with buddy,
out into the lava shift of the strobes,
out into the roiling
spree of the dance floor.

The Swallowing

Rumour is,
that one in the corner,
she's up from Georgia for the summer.
Hot, Georgia, and steamy.

Rumour is,
he was ossified;
he staggered out of the tavern and fell in the river.

Rumour is,
she laughed as they squared off, she the
proud prize for the victor, the buyer of beer.

Rumour is,
he lurched out of the beer parlour, toppled over the wharf—
the tide gave him back later.

Rumour is,
under the red-hot lights of the dance floor
she clasped him close to her; that night
they each found a way out of the surrounding dark.

Rumour is,
lots of jobs down north,
big money down north. Or
big jobs down south, lots of
money down south.

Rumour is,
he climbed up into the antlered light fixture;
when the cops came, he roared down, in his falsetto,
Watch out now—I'll gut the place!

Rumour is,
before the crash
the police stopped him twice that night,
didn't take his keys. He passed the breathalyzer,
walked a straight line.

Rumour is,
two hours later, her sons out in the car;
the ten-year-old, in the rear, deep in comics,
wriggled into the front, saved the both of them:
jammed on the brake after the three-year-old
fiddled with the gearshift, headed them out towards the water.

Rumour is,
buddy took off for the mainland;
now she's anyone's for the price of a vodka.

Rumour is,
the cocaine is crack, the poker game's fixed,
the dealer's a narc, the jukebox is broken.

Rumour is,
that one's drowning a sorrow,
that one's fleeing a demon. Here
the shadows are warming; here
there's always a story to accompany
the swallowing.

Or That's What They Say

Well, I'm a fine one to be talking about beer parlours, I'll tell you. We wouldn't venture through the doors of those places, not even if our husbands were loaded inside and we fretting and fuming hours in the cold car.

The bold ones'd send in a small youngster to ask him to come on out of it—and he might or he mightn't. But, I guarantee you, we'd as soon think of doing the Lancers on the altar as darken the door of Fureys' or Fewers'. Now a bit later on, the Velvet Horn maybe, for a dance or a wedding or something. But the beer parlours were the land of no go. No women wanted. *Pause.*

That's not to say one or two didn't—you'd see them traipsing the roads, painted up bright as a dory: Rosella and Ruby, and that one down the shore—Carmelita, Angelina, what was her name now—some saint or other, but Magdalen'd do better. Word was, they'd egg on the young fellows, half-cut when they came there, their flasks on the hip. A few crooked words, then off with the jackets, and the place'd go up. The fellow left standing, he got the girl. A few beers for Carmelita, Angelina, and then off in the dark to the back seat or the meadow.

Pause. Or that's what they say.

Tommy's Lounge

There's Western gear on Tommy's sign;
sketched Stetson, boots and star.

Here's no tang of kelp or brine,
but big bucks hauled in quick, by gar.

And, caught in a pane, a stave of lines—
and the wild wind that blows us far.

Western gear on Tommy's sign:
sketched Stetson, boots and star.

Riddling

How is a club like a story?

One may beget the other;
atmosphere is all;
the light is a transforming one;
in the shadows lurk symbols and myths;
the characters are gathered against the storm;
time stops or expands or shrinks;
epiphanies abound—or fail to occur;
the narrator is unreliable.

Darts

In a flash the hand soars into flight;
here the scuffed lino's a stage.
The bar chatter's faint from this height.

Banished from thought is the fight
that burrowed its way out of rage;
in a flash, the hand soars into flight.

Y'know, the missus and buddy are tight.
That fella stole his new gauge.
The bar chatter's faint from this height.

Birds hover or, it might be, a kite:
the plodder's transformed to a sage.
In a flash the hand soars into flight.

The wheel of the dartboard's a site
where drudgery's exiled, and age.
The bar chatter's faint from this height.

The massed shadows now cannot quite
mew up this prey in their cage.
In a flash the hand soars into flight;
the bar chatter's faint from this height.

(Re)Naming the Clubs

The Quick Hand, the Steady Eye;
The Blurring;

The Circle of Dreams;
Lord of the Dance, Cock of the Walk;

The Instigator;
The Bucket of Blood;

Lore-Hoard;
The Bunker;

Ifs and Ands;
The Twillick;

Wishes and Horses;
Swim to the Bottom;

The Sharing;
Night Refuge.

Waste Ground

...there is much more to life than meets the I.
–Ange Mlinko, "More than Meets the I"

Tansy

Athanasia, ferny,
pert, buttoned up, your
gold cardigan buttons.
Wouldn't peg you for a
necrophiliac.
Inside the corpses'
cavities you're radiant—
no sweet talk of rebirth,
just a delay,
a lingering.

Juniper

What a falling off here.
Hippocrates' crony,
soother of kidneys—
you and your demure blue.
Then the long slide
down to gutters and mothers' ruin—
that delirium, that
smouldering.

Dandelion

In your heyday a nurse—
no Miss Prim even then:
you'd get the golden stream
on the go. Heigh-ho.
It's your night self
ravishes: sphere of mist,
fairy clock,
blowballs.

Daisy

Yep, I'm the sunny one,
chirpy, day's eye,
your throwaway
love calculator,
your good luck bundle.
Wart remover, hairdresser.
Little do you care
I sprang from the Magdalen's tears,
am sown by the still-born:
ghost gift for the sorrowing.

Parsley

Hard to believe
he hangs around tombs.
They toss him compliments:
A dapper fellow—curly head—
such fresh breath.
A prince of temperance.
Still, it's whispered in
back roads and valleys
he and the Devil
are *just like that.*

Goldenrod

I, ma'am, am the upright doctor,
transmuter of silica,
Stitcher of gashes,
fixer of teeth that
wobble in gums.
Fire quencher: I lay
a cool hand on wounds,
on insect pricks.

Stinging Nettle

Burn, baby, burn.
Such acid wit—
and a spinner,
a healer. But they want
a milquetoast, cliché.
You languish in waste fields.
You're too
Jane Austen by far.

Dog Rose

I look daggers—
but it's all a pose.
I'm the old nanny, the fat cook
with my jams and jellies,
my syrups and teas.
You sneeze, and I'm
bustling, tut-tutting.

Joe Pye Weed

A wanderer in ditches,
with a homely moniker—
but—I'll come clean with you—
some call me
graveroot, purple boneset,
hint at my *gravitas.*
Bees signal their savvy,
worship around and about me.

Sorrel

Young sourpuss,
summoner of grimaces.
Blood-washer,
belly-calmer.
Your touch
might banish
the bag-lady's sores,
the squeegee boy's scabs.

Hops

Okay, so the joke's on me:
a climber, I've fallen.
Me: a king among bakers and tailors.
Morpheus' right-hand man.
Most days now
I slouch over the bar,
full of bluster,
rheumy-eyed, belching
beer-fuelled sagas.

Clover

Scuttling out,
Eve made off with me.
You'll find me where mares foal.
You think to read my leaves,
apply your puny
numbers.
Your questions.
I never yet
saved a man from the army.

Yarrow

I was Achilles' pal,
patched up his men.
My stalks counselled Druids.
I slept in muslin
under many a pillow.
Daisy troops
in my pearly roofs,
my furrowed stems feathery.
Inside my shelter
you chase after
bright eyes, a still belly.
Your gall:
so much to beg
of one you dub
thousand weed
mother-die
bad-man's plaything.

Waste Ground: Riddling

The coat hanger asks a question; the armchair is suddenly crouched…

–Don McKay, "Baler Twine"

A second skin—
my oily demeanour
between you and the weather.

◊

A miniature planet,
I glow with a watery light.
See my lines of longitude;
see my small beard
and my single green horn.

Oh you may judge it bluster,
but I'm the most stupendous of travellers!
They speak of me from the Pole to Cape Horn.
All aquiver, they dub me prima donna,
say I relish melodrama,
savour a tornado, or a good typhoon.

◊

I'm your open sesame,
your abracadabra.
Your own greedy Gollum.
Compact, rectangular,
your pal at the bazaar.
Depend on me
and I'll go for your jugular.

You dare call me drudge?
Think again, mister.
As shadows lengthen
I'm witch horse,
the scarecrow's mother,
the lurker in the corner.

◊

An old man, an infant:
my emblems.
I run through the fields like a hare.
I run my fingers through your hair.

Muscle of water.
Speckled lunge.
Anti-freeze in my blood,
iron, a gold ring and a
small pig in my belly,
I charge the depths.

◊

I'm fond of a quiet spot,
a shady nook.
Don't dare dismiss me
as greenhorn—
when lakes boiled,
when mastodons clashed,
my mother's foremothers
rode the bright air.

A pale-faced patron,
I've paid your salary.
At your table a regular.
But I harbour grim secrets:
I've served the torturer;
I've put that flush in your cheek.

◊

A jumbled alphabet,
I'm a means to your saying.
A skittering creature
at rest by my side.

I'm a cold-hearted dazzler,
an albino chameleon—
now light as a feather,
now hefty, a burden.
I warn you now:
it'll end in tears.

◊

A breathing apparatus,
I gave the Irish their letters.
Some folks cleave to me,
thwarting my killers.

Oh it's all very well—
when you're tired or you're down
you creep to my altar,
slide into my trance.
You know how
to push my buttons.
Then for days you ignore me.
One day you'll find it
harder to leave me.
It's your comfort I think of—
I squat here and wait.

◊

I'm a small bass fiddle,
cow-swallower,
king of the slime,
the plague's first note.

Coffin or cradle—
the waves decide.

◊

A rumble, a murmur.
A spring erection, rosy,
unfurling quick to
crinkly green fans.

Small as a flicker,
huge as a mountain.
Wind's my fickle friend.
Tame me, I'll serve you.
Turn your back, I'll
devour you
and all that's about you.

◊

There was a bruising at my making.
After, I seethed.
I can make folks glad;
I can steal their brains.

I am an old beast,
an ancient howl
caught in my throat.
When I utter
from my flared mouth
all the lost souls cry out.

◊

I'm a jaunty fellow,
a sparkling guest
in my thin white suit
and my jolly red hat.
Invite me in,
you'll wish you hadn't.
A convicted thief,
I'm hard to evict.

I know the secrets of trees,
but there's a terrible blank
at my heart.
Like a burnt-out comedian
I rely on others' lines.

◊

I'm invisible,
yet changeable.
I'm light as eider
and fierce as a tiger.
I've four lieutenants
to do my bidding.

You coaxed me up out of the sea—
yes, you've always needed me—
probed bowels of the earth,
all just to cull me.
I've built up vast empires.
Lethal and vital,
I'm a matter of tears.

◊

Once the woods were my home;
I had a sure footing.
Now I've learned to love flux.
Where it's all ups and downs
I'm the wind's painted plaything.

Me, a thing of wisps and flutters,
a green hand?
Guess again.
I am the ancient one,
the survivor.
I launch my messengers
all over the earth.

Triads

i
Three eyes that test mettle:
    the eye of the storm
    the eye of the needle
    a jealous eye

ii
Three emblems of limit:
    the flaw in the carpet
    the fly in the ointment
    the snake in the garden

iii
Three things that boil over:
    an unwatched pot
    the sea in wild wind
    an overwrought lover

iv
Three knots that torment:
    a knot in the hair
    a knot in the belly
    a Gordian knot

v
Three hellish holes:
    the glory hole
    the sink hole
    the pigeonhole

vi
Three things that get harder with age:
    threading a needle
    tying a knot
    untying a knot

vii
Three falls from grace:
    Churchill Falls
    Muskrat Falls
    Lucifer's fall

viii
Three myths for a time of plague:
    the sword of Damocles
    the shirt of Nessus
    Pandora's box

ix
Three eggs that arouse awe:
    a Fabergé egg
    the egg in the womb
    the Egg of the World

The Alba Poems

Sartorial

Alba noticed it was just about then
she had begun to dress like a beetle.
Before that she'd been given to
rigging herself out like a
Painted Lady or a Question Mark.
Oh she was aerial:
high wire was her mode.

The night sultry, thick with rose-smells,
a swathe around her: a pashmina
insinuating, a skin on her skin.
Wind letting loose a long riff through the aspens,
sliding in, like Flynn, silky-fingered,
quick through the wide-open window.

Now she was donning the gear
of a hunkered-down soldier—
the duns and mouse-grays,
taupes, rotted greens.
Was it a matter of camouflage
or some Jane Austen manoeuvre?
Would it tip just a bit further—
into lace collars, antimacassars,
doilies, and little skirts for the cat?

Hobby

Old hunting habits survive:
Alba's still trying
to make absence palpable.
Her blown-glass ghosts
hang in tiers on her patio.
On days windless they're pure:
steady conduits of light.
But when the wind rises,
an eerie genie,
their manner shifts with it.
First they tinkle and clink;
then there's a clashing and clatter—
is that smashing she hears—
an uproar of shards, as if
Meg March, Mary Poppins,
Goody Two-Shoes, Pollyanna,
and all the angels in the house
are running off shrieking:
their shapes overtaken now
by vampires, by succubi,
by all the witches of Eastwick.

Doppelgänger

Alba looks in the mirror,
glimpses, some days, her neighbour,
tending her hurts.

She'd started with a small plot,
acidic soil, a few stunted rhodoras,
Labrador tea mingling with lambkill.

Now she tends a large garden of grudges,
rife with nettles and thistles, goutweed
running and whispering along the borders.

Patiently, with care and with skill,
she is teaching
her daughters the art.

(With their dolls Snub and Askance
they play gooseberry,
recite the resentment rosary.)

On the north boundary
splayed like a warning
a stiff strangled mouse.

Luck

The realtor's a cooer:
"A lucky find—pure
Paradise just an hour out of town,"
she flutters, eyes eager;
"come July the whole hill
will break out in dog roses."
With a sweep of her arm
she takes in the scene.
She gestures further.
Beyond the valley before them,
off on a ridge to the west:
three horses in silhouette.
Dark and lithe
against the flaming sky.
A pure Tourist Moment.

Alba knows she's a mark,
longs to smash up
these slick stereotypes,
these tropes—to
put an arm round
this plump striver,
slip into her folksiest,
her jolliest manner:

"Sure my duck I grew up
with those cursed wild roses,
worse than the dandelions if
you're wanting a garden—
roots down to hell
with side roots to purgatory.

Knock a few thousand off
and I'll take on a rose-fight."
She'd most likely stop there—
after all the realtor's
just plying her trade.

But maybe
she'll take an axe to that idyll,
remark on the horses,
that sweet Arcady one hill over,
wonder if they've sprung from

the same stock as the twenty-odd
(Dollys and Besses and Dobbins,
to name just a few)
found charred on that ridge
one throat-tightening dawn
a century past.
A mighty night lightning had stolen
the luck stored in their shoes.

No Entry

Across a gulf Alba stares into her story,
tries to fathom that nightmare, that flight.

*

Between her and her terrorist
she's put a wide ocean.

Seven years he drummed
lover on her spine.

Her voice comes muted—
after *Salome*, *mezze*, and brandy

over a gas fire and candles
on the edge of the Irish Sea.

She has that runway look:
egret-thin, her eyes black caves.

A muted cello, her voice—
in slow chords she releases the dark.

Still no passage from that space
into the order of chiffonier, red tiles,

cats seated like Bastet,
regal on chairs.

Her candlelit cottage: a mirage
she is not permitted to enter.

Pale Tutor

After the ricochet, the zig-zag
howl running out of her head
Rose Alba saw in a flash,
indigo,
how the thin ghost
perched on the edge of her sleep
misled the mind,
mimicked a shy animal
(long gone down the dodo's road),
how that pale tutor,
subdued to a maxim,
insisted the ferns
were bound yet to
launch spores, the weather
pattern would hold.

Alba and the Crab

An amble along the beach,
sussing out starfish—
all it was meant to be—
but there one day Alba
encountered her crab lover,
Mister Karkinos.
He got his pincers into her—
his grip was legendary—
his passion soon in her every pore.

She's his anchoress now;
her body a site of long
rites of purification;
complications of
water and salt,
lotions and creams,
chemical balms.
She's possessed,
knows it in her bones—
acceding
to his litany of demands,
his insinuations.

She strokes her skull,
tenderly—perplexed,
bemused by his insistence—
reading the topography,
her dips and crevices,
searching for the code,
the way out.

Alba, Hard of Hearing

Save your sisters—
or: save your scissors?

Sorry I cried—
or: sorry I tried?

A Gift Horse in the Mouth

People renting glass houses
are out throwing stones.
In spite of their non-stop
rolling, they're gathering moss,
catching flies with vinegar—
all the while failing to
turn the other cheek.

Practice, it would seem,
doesn't make perfect.
Two birds in the bush
get on much better than
a bird in the hand.
The meek are not blessed.
A stitch in time
allows in the gremlins.
All heels inexplicably
don't find themselves wounded.

Behind that black cloud
lurks no silver lining.
It rains; it rains *and* it pours.

Words are worn thin.
Alba wants to bite the hand that feeds her,
to cut off her nose to spite her face.
She wants to look a gift horse in the mouth,
bring it to water
and damn well make it drink.

Riff

Alba's ruminating
on *fettle* and *kilter* and *trim*—
not *in fine* re *fettle* and *trim*—
and *kilter*—well, she's definitely
absolutely out of that.

Debunker

As he well might say:
nostalgia be damned.
The pain in this room
is no ache for lost home.
It's crackle, snap, crack:
junks of dry spruce in November.
A wound full of venom,
his stories burn red:
the fellow with a flat-iron—
did away with his wife. He hung for it.
The dead woman's sister, a nun, was a drunk—
and you've heard tell of
old Brennan who dug up the corpse—
she'd married the other fellow,
dropped dead a week later—
he twists toward the window,
flicks back the dimity curtain.
And where's that one prancing off to now?
What's that he's got in his hands?
It's salmon. Two big chunks of salmon.
The ungrateful bastard.

Listening, tranced,
prim Alba catalogues what
she's gleaned on her summer
vacation:
young earwigs hang out in pine cones,
pine cones ready to sail out from the tree;
winter mice, starving, will
gnaw holes in linen, sensing

the frail ghost of flax;
Coney Island seagulls will
scoop ice cream right out of the cone,
will swoop down, lightning-beaked,
and snatch it right out of your hand.

She clutches her hands,
loosens them,
clutches again—
as if the left could comfort the right,
as if the right could comfort the left.
As if time could fold over on itself
and open into a white crane in flight.

Her Seer Hat On

What her crystal ball told her,
grumbling and swirling:

The charred forests will reach up,
sway leafy arms to the sky.

Salmon will crowd the falls,
tails lashing, blood running.

Sea-birds will unoil
themselves, the beaches washed clean.

Croesus—and his ilk—call
stolen billions home from offshore.

Each table will groan, laden
with bread, milk, and *honey.*

A chicken in every pot,
a shelter for every head.

Poilievre and his sack of poison
will vanish in a puff of smoke.

Clear heads will prevail:
vaccines in every arm.

Celeb babble and other baby talk
will—poof!—be gone from the airwaves.

The Muses, lithe, will sashay on in,
the listeners all gladdened:

no more dancing attendance
on truism, shibboleth, tiresome cliché.

A buzzing, an electronic sizzling,
a hiss. Alba's globe turned opaque.

Alba's Scrapbook

Alba's been pasting in her rose-bordered
scrapbook words they once used
to beat women with:
slattern and *spinster* and *slut.*
So much sibilance. Was it
a sort of sympathetic magic, a
hissing meant to usurp
powers of the great mothers,
huge snakes coiling all blue and
iridescent, indifferent under the
lacerating sun?

Now Alba comes up with her own spitting list:
slieveen, and *shyster.*
Scoundrel and *sook.*
No nimbus here of house-
keeping or sex
(tidy legs crossed),
rather
an invoking of, no,
an exacting of
straight-dealing and blood-sport.

Punctuation Marks

Time's pricking.
Dead ends, escape hatches.

If Alba were one, she'd be
an ellipsis—or maybe
a dash.
A wandering current or a waterfall.

She watches the
exclamation points
thronging around her—
feels her gorge rise,
bile burn in her throat.

Semi-colons and
question marks
shadowing
the philosophers' moves,
the politicians'.
(The connections are dubious.)

But for the most part
a vastness of commas, those
flabby traffic cops who on the sly
are peddling drugs, *and then*,
and then, *and then*.

Alba keeps looking out for
the trumpeter, courtly:
the colon—or else that

prince of ambivalence,
the interrobang.

Though it's fair to say
that on the whole
these days
she's glimpsing down alleys,
and round cosy street corners,
the magisterial,
firm-handed, top-hatted
Mr. Period—
full stop.

Still
she's not cried uncle,
conceded the game,
given up the ghost.
O no not yet.
She's setting up to
slip inside and away, via
the first likely parenthesis
that happens along.

Terms of Endearment

Alba's been thinking
about terms of address.
Dear, honey, sweetie,
my dear.
Marooned in Emergency, prone,
through the thin cotton curtains pulled round
she hears the unctuous
tones, the sobriquets which
put the older among us
firmly in place, that is to say
in a crib, the supposed
endearments rendering
them infants, imbeciles.

Alba's got her own woes; she too's
at the mercy of these so-casual
putdowns as she waits
for her assembly-line once-over.

She wants to rear up on her hind legs,
roar through the drapery, shout out
to these scurrying figures, *That's*
Doctor Wareham to you, and she has
more knowledge in her little finger
than you'll amass in your Facebook-
addled lifetime.

And that trembly old fellow you're
quizzing as if he were brain-dead,
he's steered ships with a surgeon's hand;

delivered triplets in a blackout;
knows the tricks and manners of tides
and the phases of the moon. Is these days
the lynchpin of his clan and his town.

Alba and the Good Friday Cat

He was a walking crucifixion,
the eyes on him a glass you didn't
want to look into.
Mueck's giant, hunched
and staring in his corner.
A coat that marked him
kin to the clerk in Gogol:
lead gray, dulled
by now-and-then feeding,
by car grease and clay.

Alba watched him,
wary on her stoop.
An ink-slash cloud in the sky.
The day a festival of
man's inhumanity to man.
The radio playing
its symphony of murder:
bass notes for the occasion.
Alba shivered in her
thin coat of cotton,
last night's supper
and her brother's story
drifting into mind.

Her brother told her:
This fellow couldn't hold a job, see,
something gone wrong with his brain.
And his gums were going,
so the dentist told him;

ordered him off to the peri-
odontist.
Buddy called up the Welfare
and this is what he heard:

for the ones with bad luck,
bad karma, bad vibes,
the diabetic, pathetic,
the psychotic, rheumatic,
schizophrenic, allergic,
the smashed-up by a bus or a moose—
for the ones down the rabbit hole
who fell through the cracks,
missed out on the good genes,
the fast-earning portfolio,
the ones who don't, can't, won't
bring home the bacon,

we've got a special arrangement,
a super-duper tooth solution.
We've a handy-dandy remedy,
economical and neat.
It's a dilly, a doozie,
why, it's such a clever
contrivance, a
one-size-fits-all plan.

When your chompers give you trouble,
and your gums are screaming red,
we'll be there on the double,
fix that aching in your head—
then *the dollars we'll fork over—*
so a doc can haul your teeth.

No cleanings, and no fillings,
oh no drillings, dear, for you,
no root canals, no implants—
that buck-demanding jazz—
but oh if there's a crisis,
why then we've judged it proper
for a doc to yank your teeth.

That way we'll keep our borders strong
between those rich and poor—
politicos: slick pearly smiles,
mouths sunken for the poor.

Alba slid a saucer out to the cat;
he edged nearer, slow, sullen,
lapped up the meaty slop,
slinked off through a gap.
For Alba now
it was off to the Basilica looming
under the charcoal sky.

The Old Woman and Alba

Alba scoffed at the notion of ghosts,
thought them a trick of the neurons,
a drift of the light, or a dream.

But the old woman's persistence
brought her up short—
that and the state of her:

ragged skirts, a gauze of grime
all about her: a clutch of fraying
papers in her lean mottled hands.

And her keening voice, a voice
that would wake the dead:
demos, cratos, demos, cratos—

her chant was relentless,
a litany laden with
the torment and twisting of ages.

Alba felt the chill
rippling all down along her neck,
felt the shiver, the hairs rise.

What did the old crone want,
this tottering
bundle of old clothes

and lament, her
visits more frequent,
her cries growing louder?

Now she seemed to be morphing
into some sort of demented clown,
juggling letters of a wooden alphabet;

up she'd pop, just when
Alba'd burrowed into *The Telegram,*
or sat drowsing over the late-night news.

She was shifty, full of stratagems:
this week it was placards,
cobbled together out of old campaign posters,

tilted aloft in those scrawny old arms.
What is a library? read one,
edged with a chain of interlinked hands.

What is a school? read another;
Who knows best? Can you spell despot*?*
She had Alba moithered.

And now the ghost was bringing her cronies along;
Alba caught glimpses of
Armine Gosling, Cleisthenes, and Nellie McClung.

The Toms: Douglas and Paine;
Pankhurst and Parnell,
Mandela, Havel. What a din.

One stormy evening the wraith
waltzed with Ray Guy round her room—the pair
moaning and shrieking like demons in agony.

...

Alba's resigned now:
the old dame *will* have her say.
Next time she shows up

Alba'll be ready to set off at her side—
with questions, wry hope;
with a sharp pen, a history book;

with counterpoints and suggestions;
with commitment and queries;
and her best protest shoes.

What Came

Awkward Alba, hunched over
a battered oak desk. Rain
riffing easy along the roof;
then a lunatic moon shedding its grief
through the window. She
was, it might be, setting out
in a spell words that would net
a glimpse, or faint spoor,
of the shy beast named Love.

She was expecting Cupid to drop in,
that petulant boy, so careless
with toys. Or Aengus,
dreamy-eyed after travels. Or—
spell gone awry—maybe
Heathcliff, or Dracula, cape flung back
to flaunt the red lining
as thunder roared, bolts carved up the sky.

What came, though, was quieter:
the arc of a hand as it pulled
thread through a needle, wielded
a paintbrush on walls of a sickroom;
a shoulder taut in the hoisting
a bed frame, wrought-iron, up stairs.

ACKNOWLEDGEMENTS

Thanks to the editors of the following journals, magazines, and anthologies in which some of these poems have appeared, occasionally in slightly different versions: *The Fiddlehead, Horseshoe, MacLean's, Newfoundland Quarterly, Riddle Fence; The Democracy Cookbook: Recipes to Renew Governance in Newfoundland and Labrador.*

The opening section, "Taking Stock," is forthcoming from Memorial University Press in the multi-genre anthology *Corner Stor(i)es*, edited by Michelle Porter.

"All the Clubs from Holyrood to Brigus: Fictions, Ruminations, and Riddles" appeared in the art catalogue *All the Clubs from Holyrood to Brigus.* It accompanied an exhibition of photographs by Scott Walden, mounted at the Sir Wilfred Grenfell College Art Gallery.

The poems of "Waste Ground" were published as a letterpress limited-edition chapbook by Marnie Parsons of Running the Goat Books and Broadsides, with illustrations by engraver Abigail Rorer.

"Sartorial" was originally published on the website of Parliamentary Poet Laureate John Steffler.

My thanks to all involved in bringing this work to readers—especially to editor Carmine Starnino, for shepherding *Interrobang* into print.

My gratitude also to those whose memories inspired some of the images in "Taking Stock" and "All the Clubs from Holyrood to Brigus": John Byrne, Joseph Byrne, Anne Dalton, John Dalton, Margaret Dalton, Pad Dalton, David Woodman; and to Scott Walden whose invitation to write an essay about his club photos led me to poems instead.

NOTES

TAKING STOCK

"The Shop": Biscuit-box houses are a traditional form of Newfoundland architecture. Named after the rectangular boxes used to ship hard biscuits (hard tack), these two-storey houses had very slightly sloping roofs.

"Gerald S. Doyle's Cod Liver Oil: The Blue Bottle": These title words appear on the bottle's label; they appear also on stationery and ads.

So pure and so strong occurs in the refrain of a popular comic ballad of the time:

> Oh doctor, oh doctor, oh dear Doctor John
> your cod liver oil is so pure and so strong
> I'm afraid of my life, I'll go down in the soil
> If me wife don't stop drinking your cod liver oil
> –"Cod Liver Oil"

"Anti-Costco (Shopping List)": Cabbage garden was the name given to the small mixed gardens cultivated close to houses, tended by women, as distinct from the much larger gardens full of potatoes and other root vegetables, and, like the hay meadows, cultivated at a distance from the house and tended by men and women both, as needed.

"Anti-Costco (By size)": The image of a bow-tied black terrier appeared on each Scotty's chip bag.

ALL THE CLUBS FROM HOLYROOD TO BRIGUS

The numbers attached to the titles of the following pieces indicate that the particular poem is a direct response to that numbered Walden photograph in the series: "Girl at the Bar" #24; "Tommy's Lounge" #47; "Darts" #7.

Walden's entire series can be seen at: scottwalden.net/clubs

WASTE GROUND

"Parsley": Parsley, is, course, an escaped domestic here, hanging with the outliers, as suits his devilish temperament.

TRIADS

The use of the triad form can be found in societies worldwide, but was particularly common in Celtic-influenced areas. The triads I've created are in the tradition of mediaeval Irish ones, which encompassed a wide range of subjects and tones. Many encapsulate rules of law or community etiquette; others were carriers of history, geography, botany, genealogy, medical lore, as well as of life wisdom. A famous translation of these is scholar Kuno Meyer's *The Triads of Ireland.*

THE ALBA POEMS

"Doppelganger": In Newfoundland one name for blueberries is 'hurts.'

"The Old Woman and Alba": The old woman is a figure of democracy under threat. At the time of my writing this piece, the government of Newfoundland and Labrador had announced its intention to close several libraries across the province; at the same time it was making announcements about closing schools and bussing students long distances. The public outcry about libraries was so great that the government reversed its decision; struggles about schools continue, and libraries are underfunded.

Ray Guy was a satirist and humorist whose newspaper columns were a political force in Newfoundland.

Signal
EDITIONS

CARMINE STARNINO, EDITOR
MICHAEL HARRIS, FOUNDING EDITOR

Robert Allen • James Arthur • John Asfour, trans.
John Barton • Doug Beardsley • Paul Bélanger
Linda Besner • Walid Bitar • Marie-Claire Blais
Yves Boisvert • Jenny Boychuk • Asa Boxer • Susan Briscoe
René Brisebois, trans. • Mark Callanan • Chad Campbell
Edward Carson • Arthur Clark • Yoyo Comay
Don Coles • Vincent Colistro • Jan Conn • Geoffrey Cook
Lissa Cowan, trans. • Judith Cowan, trans. • Mary Dalton
Ann Diamond • George Ellenbogen • Louise Fabiani
Joe Fiorito • Bill Furey • Michel Garneau • Susan Glickman
Gérald Godin • Lorna Goodison • Richard Greene
Jason Guriel • Michael Harris • Carla Hartsfield
Elisabeth Harvor • Charlotte Hussey • Dean Irvine, ed.
Jim Johnstone • D.G. Jones • Francis R. Jones, trans.
Virginia Konchan • Anita Lahey • Kateri Lanthier
R. P. LaRose • Ross Leckie • Erik Lindner • Michael Lista
Laura Lush • Errol MacDonald • Brent MacLaine
Muhammad al-Maghut • Nyla Matuk • Robert McGee
Sadiqa de Meijer • Robert Melançon • Robert Moore
Pierre Morency • Pierre Nepveu • Eric Ormsby
Elise Partridge • Christopher Patton • James Pollock
Michael Prior • Medrie Purdham • John Reibetanz
Peter Richardson • Robin Richardson • Laura Ritland
Talya Rubin • Richard Sanger • Stephen Scobie

Talya Rubin • Richard Sanger • Stephen Scobie
Peter Dale Scott • Deena Kara Shaffer
Carmine Starnino • Andrew Steinmetz • David Solway
Ricardo Sternberg • Shannon Stewart
Philip Stratford, trans. • Matthew Sweeney
Harry Thurston • Rhea Tregebov • Peter Van Toorn
Patrick Warner • Derek Webster • Anne Wilkinson
Donald Winkler, trans. • Shoshanna Wingate
Christopher Wiseman • Catriona Wright
Terence Young